The Crypto Kid

A Guide to Understanding the Basics of Crypto and the Mindset of a Successful Investor

Published by: The Ghost Publishing, LLC
Author: Jackson Shembekar
Editor: Eli Gonzalez
Contact info: jrshembekar@icloud.com
Cover Design: The Ghost Publishing, LLC

B

To my mother,
for her love, support, confidence and countless hours
with me.

To
Preston & Colin,
who are not only my brothers,
but also
My Best Friends.

Special acknowledgment to:

Coach Terry Rupp for
Seeing Potential in Me

Without meeting Nick Indelicato
this Book would not have been Possible

Jesuit High School
Thank you for the endless opportunities. You brought me into a
space which encapsulated the highest form of education, the
finest musical program, and a national sports team.

Testimonials

"You can't go wrong following The Crypto Kid. Not only does he teach about cryptocurrency and the tendencies of an investor, but Jackson Shembekar will also motivate you to do better in every aspect of your life."

Kevin Harrington, Original Shark on Shark Tank,
Inventor of the Infomercial

"The cryptocurrency world can be very complex, scary even, which is why I recommend The Crypto Kid to anyone considering to invest. Jackson Shembekar has proven to understand this new and still-forming landscape like a true veteran."

Raymond Hyer, Asphalt Industry Leader, Philanthropist

"Jackson Shembekar is a leading voice in this growing world of cryptocurrency and the global economy. His story is captivating and is a great read for anyone looking to learn."

Jugal Taneja, Venture Capitalist, Philanthropist

"The cryptocurrency marketplace is complex and rapidly evolving. In 'The Crypto Kid,' Jackson Shembekar provides an insightful and fascinating introduction based on his personal experience and success navigating the cryptocurrency world."

Don Grava, Founder and President of Versailles Group

Table of Contents

INTRODUCTION

I Love What I Do

As I write this, I'm at the end of my high school career preparing to embark on a new journey to play college baseball. Over the last four years, I have specialized in a unique financial subset originating back to only 2008 - cryptocurrency. And I've already made a million dollars in the industry. What's not to love?

As you read this book, you'll see that I'm a logical thinker. Expressing my feelings or showing my passion is not something that comes easily to me. However, that being said, I want to impress upon you how excited and exuberant I am that I found out about cryptocurrency when I did. It has already changed my life.

There are many things I love about cryptocurrency. It's relatively new, it's highly sought after, and clearly, it's been very lucrative for me. But, above all, it allows people a new avenue to achieve financial freedom.

Cryptocurrency is here to stay. In fact, I believe that decentralized finance as a whole will revolutionize the existing financial infrastructure in less than twenty years. If you don't get involved now, you will miss out on the biggest technological innovation since the internet.

The Root of All Evil

Sadly, many people believe that the root of all evil is money. But that's not true. Rather, it's greed - the excessive desire of money. It is only when you would do anything to anyone, regardless of principles or morals, that money becomes a bad thing. The fact is, money only amplifies the character in each and every one of us.

Like every other nation, India was ravaged by COVID-19. India actually suffered more than most countries. In an act of amazing humanitarianism, Vitalik Buterin, the founder of Ethereum (the second largest cryptocurrency), donated one billion dollars to provide aid to the people of India. With that single gesture, he literally saved thousands of lives. That's the power of giving. That's the power of money.

When people ask me for advice on cryptocurrency, whether it's a classmate, a political figure, an executive, or even a major league baseball player, I always give them the same book. It's an easy read of less than one hundred pages. I've personally given the same copy to more than thirty people. It baffles me that most of them who have had the book in their possession for an extended period of time have never even read it. For those who actually did take the plunge, investing a miniscule amount of time to learn, they did extremely well. They'd text me questions, I'd give them answers, and they'd execute.

I've personally advised top executives and highly successful individuals with net worths upwards of One Billion Dollars. I've also advised broke high school and college students. If anyone wanted to know how to get into cryptocurrency, I was more than willing to offer my time.

This Book

It was never my intention to write a book of my own. However, when people heard how I started out with a twenty dollar investment and built up to a seven-figure portfolio in less than four years, they had to know how I did it. When the tangible results began to realize themselves at an exponential pace, my mother convinced me to share my story. The result is the book you're holding in your hands.

Before you jump headfirst into this book, understand that cryptocurrency is laden with new language – new jargon, if you will. It's a new currency founded on a new way of thinking. New coins and new ideas continuously pop up. You may read newly invented words or phrasings that are hard to comprehend, but I've done everything I can to simplify the blockchain world while still informing you of everything you need to know to become successful in the industry.

My hope for this book is that it changes people's lives for the better. I hope it falls into the hands of someone who was forced to drop out of college because they couldn't afford it. I hope it falls into the hands of someone in a third world country who thinks he or she is destined to live a life beyond poverty. In essence, I hope that this book helps people all over the world, across all walks of life, understand that they don't have to stay stuck in a rut forever. With some patience, training, and boldness you too can become financially free.

Most importantly, since this book has fallen into your hands, I hope that it inspires you. You are capable of living the life you desire. It might just be one trade away.

CHAPTER 1
Time is Money

The Most Important Thing in the World

What's the most important thing in the world to you? Often, the answer I hear is family. That answer resonates to the core of my being. As you'll read later, I didn't have the traditional family upbringing. However, there is nothing I wouldn't do for my mother or my brothers. Family is everything to me. But, family is a cop out answer.

The real answer, in my opinion, is Time. Time is the quintessential untradeable asset we have. I want more time on this planet, more time with my family, more time to pursue my goals, more time to build a legacy, and more time to experience this one-of-a-kind thing called life.

Time waits for no one. It doesn't ask for permission. It just keeps with its linear continuum, regardless of what you are doing with it. In fact, it won't even notice when you've run out of it. Time is a horrible taskmaster. However, if you can master it, the sky is the limit.

As of the writing of this book, I'm a senior in high school. I play the piano. I play the violin. I'm an A student. I'm a pilot. I play baseball. I work out. I hang out with my friends. And I watch movies. But most importantly, I'm in the top 1% of the global population when it comes to cryptocurrency holdings. I don't say this to boast. I write this in hopes of challenging you to take control of your time. When people ask me how I've been able to do what I've done in a relatively few amount of years, I say that I've learned how to make time work for me.

Collect the Outs

I've been playing baseball since I was 10. It's part of my DNA now. I love to play, I love to compete, and I love to test myself against the best. As a pitcher, my only goal is to throw the baseball toward the catcher with the intention of retiring the batter. The complexity is often drawn out with velocity, command, tempo, cadence, pitch selection, and a multitude of other factors; but, the only real objective is to collect an out.

You may have picked up this book to learn more about cryptocurrency, but at a deeper level, I think what you'll also find is that you need to be awakened from your walking slumber. There is a destiny inside of you that's far beyond what you've probably imagined. Unfortunately, it's trapped under a basement guarded by FEAR.

Fear is the result of a lack of preparation. If you're prepared, there's no reason to be fearful. Sure, it's okay to be nervous, but that's different from feeling fear. When it comes to investing, I have no fear.

Now, don't get me wrong, fear is a useful and valuable emotion. It's kept us safe since the dawn of humanity. It's what has saved many of us from embarrassing moments, monumental failures, and existing danger. The problem arises when fear leaves its borders and invades other parts of your life. When fear keeps you at your status quo, it holds you back from taking the necessary risks to become the best that you can be.

Fear of failure, of not being enough, and of looking foolish in front of others is, in my opinion, the number one thing that holds people back from living the life of their dreams. So, they stick to what they know, work their salary job, and portray a life much more glamorous than their reality. In terms of living your dreams and becoming financially independent, Kevin O'Leary, also known as

Mr. Wonderful from the hit show Shark Tank, says it best, "A salary is the drug they give you to forget your dreams."

Fear of failure, of not being enough, and of looking foolish in front of others is, in my opinion, the number one thing that holds people back from living the life of their dreams. So, they stick to what they know, work their salary job, and portray a life much more glamorous than their reality. In terms of living your dreams and becoming financially independent, Kevin O'Leary, also known as Mr. Wonderful from the hit show Shark Tank, says it best, "A salary is the drug they give you to forget your dreams."

If I told you there was a way you could become financially independent, it wouldn't do anything for you. However, if I got you to truly believe there was a way you could become financially independent, that's a totally different ballgame. That could change your life! I'm going to do my part and tell you, but it's going to be up to you to believe it and take action.

I must speak plainly. I know I'm young, but I've accomplished much in my few years. You may have taken two or three times the amount of trips around the sun than me. I get it. But respectfully, I need to say this: as you embark on reading this book, turn off that little voice in your head that says "no" to anything new.

You may know something about crypto, and that's great, but let go of the arrogant epicenter of your mind, no matter how big or small, that assumes you can't learn anything new. Also, step away from any bias you may have already formulated in your mind. Relinquish control and read this book knowing that you have nothing to lose, yet everything to gain. If you read it with an open mind, you'll find that you read something you needed to learn. This book is, after all, about our futures... yours and mine.

We are at the precipice of a global financial disruption of epic proportions. In a few short decades or less, finance as we know it will be reinvented. This shouldn't come as a surprise or sound like part of a science fiction, futuristic prophecy. Humankind has experienced financial evolutions before.

The History of Money

Commerce began as simple bartering: exchanging goods or services for other goods or services — give me this and I'll give you that, give me those and I'll do this thing. Around 5,000 BC, bartering was disrupted as metal objects began to be seen as valuable. However, it was not until 700 BC that civilizations began to make coins. The invention was revolutionary. These coins were durable, difficult to counterfeit, and held intrinsic value. There was just one problem — if you had a lot, they got heavy.

This system was viable and much more effective than the bartering system, but it was still inefficient. As a result, people began to leave their coins with a trustworthy agent and were given a receipt. The receipt itself could then be traded for goods and the seller could redeem the receipt for the coins. The government soon took control of the process, and paper money was born.

Paper money began to take off. It was used globally and solved the existing problem of the coins' excessive weight. However, the paper always represented something. Whether it was gold, silver, platinum, or palladium it was symbolic. That is until the United States went off the gold standard for first the time in 1933, and when President Nixon later cut all ties to paper money representing gold in 1971.

Money is no longer backed by anything tangible. The money you and I have today in our wallets is only valuable because of the trust the general public puts in the government.

We've come a long way from trading cow milk for firewood. However, just as we've transitioned from bartering to paper money, currency is once again in the process of going through another seismic shift. The best part is that you not only have a chance to play a role in it, but you get to capitalize on it.

Cryptocurrency is here, and it's going to take over. Much like time, it doesn't care if you like it or not. But, like time, it will change your life if you learn how to master it.

Missed Opportunities

In the modern era, the 1950s to today, everyone has had opportunities to invest in many companies that would have made them rich today. The stock market is full of "rags to riches" stories. I often hear people older than me lament on missing out on investing in Microsoft, Amazon, and Yahoo! "If only I could turn back time...."

I genuinely can't stand when people don't take action in the moment, and later say, "If only I would have...." I much prefer to hear that someone took a chance at greatness and fell short. Only those that take chances in the financial world are the ones that truly impact others and are looked up to with admiration. Opportunities present themselves to anyone and everyone — all you have to do is look.

If you are reading this book, I believe that this is your chance to surpass every other investment opportunity in the entirety of your life. You are at the dawn of a once-in-a-generation opportunity. During all the evolutions of money and investments, geographical borders, language barriers, and oceans have hindered people across the globe from participating. That's not the case anymore. The internet bypasses all of these obstacles enabling anybody to get involved.

With this new, never-before-imagined reality comes a never-before-imagined clamor for a global currency. The opportunity at hand is not for the rich nor for the poor; it is for those forward thinkers who want the ball in their own hands to throw out the game's first pitch.

It's not too late to get into Cryptocurrency. As of this writing, just about every week, the market is setting a new all-time high. If you get in the game, follow my instruction, and stay the course, you're going to be much better off.

In this book are the answers you've been searching for. When you turn the page, I'm going to share with you how I turned an initial $20 investment into a seven-figure portfolio. As you read, I hope to impart to you a lesson my mother has taught me since I was a child, "Whatever you decide to do, give it your all!"

There are three types of people who will read this book:

1. Those who are scared to step in the batter's box with fear of getting hit by a pitch. These are the people who get left behind by their peers and kick themselves. These are the "If I could just turn back time..." kind of people.

2. Those who are indifferent. Their minds are made up – crypto is too new, crypto is too old, the author of this book is too young – and will not objectively give this book a chance. If that's you, please, put the book down and gift it to somebody willing to take a swing.

3. Those who know they deserve more out of life and are determined to make their time on Earth count. They don't let fear cripple them. They step up to the plate and swing for the fences.

Which one are you? Your financial situation is your personal responsibility. Stop making excuses and listen to your future self. The time to take your future into your own hands will never be better than it is now. Take control of your financial destiny. Step up to the mound and throw your best pitch. Let's play ball!

CHAPTER 2
My Story

Be Overconfident

I was quite a reserved person in middle school. If you were to have seen me at the time, you'd notice that I was six feet tall and wildly un-athletic. I had a few close friends, but I spent most of my time with my family and on self-development: piano lessons, baseball practices, basketball games, and straight A's. I've always been a driven person.

With my mother coaching and guiding me since I was little, I always put in the necessary work and effort to become the best in everything I did. The result was that I tested in the 99th percentile in middle school. As for athletics, I, who had been the last pick on the baseball team a few years prior, had developed into a decent pitcher. With my perfect grades and newfound athletic prowess behind me, my baseball coach, the legendary Terry Rupp, spoke with my mother regarding my plans for the future. He told her I'd be a great fit for Tampa Jesuit, a highly challenging academic high school with a nationally ranked baseball team. When we learned more about Jesuit and its rich history, we decided that Coach Rupp was right on the money.

Prior to my freshman year, I had to take an entrance exam to get into Jesuit. If I scored poorly in anything, I would have had to go to Summer School. I, being at the top of my class in middle school, was not very worried about the exam. I was extremely strong in math, which showed; and I thought I was strong in English as well. However, I wasn't quite at the level required by Jesuit High School.

Summer School, presented to me in the form of "Summer Enrichment", turned out to be great for me. I realized one of the primary reasons they put me there was to get me acclimated to the new surroundings and meet new people. Looking back, I'm glad I went through it.

Over that summer, my English teacher, Mr. Austin Freeman, gave me a great piece of advice - "Be overconfident." In retrospect, it was the single most important thing I learned all summer. So, on the very first day of school, when teachers came out with tiny tricycles meant for toddlers and declared it Mario Kart Monday asking, "Who wants to race?" I, being "overconfident", raised my hand. Moments later, I squeezed my six-foot frame onto a tricycle no taller than my knee and awkwardly raced around the lunchroom while students cheered, laughed, and roared. Needless to say, after the race, I was no longer an unknown. Everyone knew my name.

From 20 to a Million

Being that I'm still in high school, the story of my life is just unfolding. However, meeting Nick Indelicato could very well end up being the most financially significant moment of my life. I met Nick my freshman year in orchestra class.

Nick seemed normal at first glance, even average. But he was far beyond average – he was brilliant. Nick scored within the 99th percentile on his SAT, achieved a perfect GPA throughout high school, and is currently developing super capacitor technologies that increase sustainability on our planet.

Nick and I got to talking and he said, "I know this is going to sound cliché, but cryptocurrency is going to be the next Amazon."

I told him I'd only heard of Bitcoin, but that was the extent of my knowledge of crypto.

"Bitcoin is the one everyone is familiar with, but I'm currently trading with a smaller coin."

"What coin?" I asked.

"XRP. It's the third biggest coin right now. I bought it at twenty-five cents and it's now at three dollars. I made twelve times my investment!".

It was at that moment that it became clear to me that there was a whole new world that I knew nothing about. My curiosity ran wild for the rest of the day, and I knew I had to learn more.

(So that we're all on the same page: Bitcoin is a coin in the world of cryptocurrency. There are many other coins such as XRP; Bitcoin is simply the first, biggest, and most well known.)

My mother made sure to instill a passion for excelling in us, so I was not unfamiliar with the vigor required to truly succeed within a new skillset. When I got home that day, I started to look into this world of make-believe where a high school kid can make 1200% in just a couple of trades. Early in my investigative phase, I got hooked. I looked up YouTube videos like my life depended on it and was in awe at all the free advice right at my fingertips. It soon became my conversation of choice with Nick and my family.

I quickly made my first purchase of $20. I was all too excited to tell Nick that now, I too was a trader like him!

"Good for you, Jackson!"

When I told my mom I had put money into cryptocurrency, she challenged me, "You put in $20? If you win something, all you'll make is maybe enough money to pay for your school lunch for a day. Do more research on it, and if you feel that you are confident, go all in!"

I told Nick what my mother had told me, and he said that she was absolutely correct. "You're a smart kid, Jackson. If you put in the time to learn this skillset, you can do some real damage."

I doubled down on studying cryptocurrency. I read books, listened to podcasts, and followed veterans in the industry as if they were celebrities. Rather quickly, the language that seemed foreign at first became second nature, and the charts that looked like they had an infinite complexity to them suddenly became easier to understand.

My investment total reached $500, and the numbers began to dance for me. I told my younger brothers Preston and Colin about it, and they quickly got in my crypto corner, adding to the confidence that was starting to build. Whenever I made money, I'd reinvest it. I'd win, lose a little, win again, lose a lot, and win some more.

Had it not been for my mother, cryptocurrency could have consumed me. She never let me lose sight of the totality and diversity that makes up a dynamic individual. I now had two competitive joys in my life, playing baseball and investing in cryptocurrency.

All In

My mother, who I've referenced a few times already, is extremely good at what she does. I'll tell you the story later of her divorce and how it affected our family, but I want to stay on point with how I made a million dollars before starting college. She works in real estate, and to say that she has a knack for hidden gems in the market is a massive understatement. She has earned the trust of countless real estate investors who buy properties sight unseen. All they have is her word that they'll make money on their investment, and they do... every single time.

My brothers and I were given a unique opportunity at a young age. If we were able to close a deal – that is have an investor sign a real contract in regards to a property, we would be given a $1,500 incentive. We looked at this opportunity as a game, and it wasn't long until the competitive aspect naturally began to increase results for all three of us. This taught my brothers and me the value of a referral at a young age.

I had gotten to a point in understanding the crypto market where I was more than ready to go all in. I was no longer interested in lunch money. My sights were set on something much larger. Gone were the days of picking up the crumbs from the real investors; I was ready for the whole pie. The only problem was that much of the money my brothers and I had earned was pooled together. I had my eyes on some coins that I knew deep down were about to provide monumental returns, but I couldn't invest the type of money I wanted to without the approval of my brothers.

I spoke with Preston, who had been watching me obsess over trading for a couple of months now and asked him his plans with the money. He was an intuitive guy, so he got right to the point, "How much do you want to invest?"

When I told him the amount I wanted to invest, I thought he'd laugh or even just walk away. Instead, he replied with something I never thought he'd say: "You're the smartest guy I know. If you think this is what we should do, let's do it".

With Preston now by my side, I excitedly asked our mother if it was ok. She replied, "When I say to go all in, I don't say it just to say it. You've put in the work, you've already made some decent money, so if you're truly as confident as you appear to be, go for it." And that's exactly what I did.

I spoke with Preston, who had been watching me obsess over trading for a couple of months now and asked him his plans with the money. He was an intuitive guy, so he got right to the point, "How much do you want to invest?"

When I told him the amount I wanted to invest, I thought he'd laugh or even just walk away. Instead, he replied with something I never thought he'd say: "You're the smartest guy I know. If you think this is what we should do, let's do it".

With Preston now by my side, I excitedly asked our mother if it was ok. She replied, "When I say to go all in, I don't say it just to say it. You've put in the work, you've already made some decent money, so if you're truly as confident as you appear to be, go for it." And that's exactly what I did.

I began to put more and more money into cryptocurrency. When the market went down, I only saw it as an opportunity to invest more, and when the market went up, that's when I really began to comprehend the true depths of what I was achieving. What started out as a twenty-dollar investment, quickly grew to over fifty thousand dollars before the end of my first semester in high school!

In no way am I saying that it was all smooth sailing from there. At times, the portfolio fell below that figure, drastically even sometimes. But my consistency prevailed. I'm sure there are others that wouldn't have thought twice about cutting their losses and getting out. But not me. All the low points did was make the high points that much higher. And soon enough, the numbers started going up. I watched as my portfolio began adding zeros, until it eventually reached the coveted seven figure mark.

Now, I want to share a secret with you. One of my goals is that when I get to $2 million, I will buy my friend Nick Indelicato, the person who introduced me to this wonderful world of cryptocurrency, a Tesla. And guess what, it'll be paid for with Bitcoin.

I say all this not simply to inform you of my story, but rather so you too can embark upon your crypto journey and begin to write your own story. My goal here is to share what I know about cryptocurrency, and not just create generational wealth for my family and myself, but show you that you can too.

CHAPTER 3
What is Cryptocurrency?

Cryptocurrency

If you're reading this book, chances are you want to know what cryptocurrency is all about. By definition, cryptocurrency is simply a digital currency in which transactions are verified and maintained by a decentralized system using cryptography. The problem is that while you probably understand what those words mean, that definition, filled with buzz words, doesn't paint a good picture of what exactly cryptocurrency is and why it's important. So, allow me to try to explain it.

Before I do that though, I would like to say that you don't need to know what cryptocurrency is. You can very easily become a passive investor in crypto markets and not have an in depth understanding of how it all works. Take credit cards, for example. There's a good chance you use a credit card, but do you actually know how credit card companies work? Do you know the different factors that go into forming an individual's credit score? Now, there may be a chance that some of you reading this do know the answer to those questions, but my point is that this knowledge-based barrier to entry in crypto is a facade when it comes to passive investing.

So, assuming that you're here to learn about cryptocurrency either for the sake of pure intellectual growth or to lay the foundation for active trading in the crypto space, let's jump right into it.

Fiat Currency

To properly understand cryptocurrency, you need to first understand what exactly fiat currency is. Fiat currency is currency issued by government that is not backed by any commodity. For example, the U.S. Dollar is a fiat currency as it is controlled by the federal reserve and is no longer backed by gold.

Fiat currency has two major drawbacks.

1. It is centralized, meaning a government or banks controls it.
2. It is not limited by quantity, meaning that the government or bank that controls it can print as much as they want.

With the flaws of fiat money not going away any time soon, a shift was inevitable, but very difficult to achieve. The problem arises due to the disparity of power between the citizen and the government. The government holds power and controls the money supply with the understanding that the citizen's best interest should be kept at heart. Although, the government and the citizen often have different interests in mind. This is where the conflict begins.

Excessive money printing is a concept most citizens would agree is bad for the economy, as it directly results in inflation. But excessive money printing also lowers governmental debt providing incentive for the government. This example highlights the problems with fiat money and stresses why the move to a decentralized system was inevitable. Our systems have evolved digitally in the sense of online banking, credit cards, wires, PayPal, and more, but many of the aforementioned problems are yet to be solved because all these systems still revolve around a fiat currency.

As a result, digital currency began as an alternative. Digital currency was designed to solve corruption, theft, inflation, incompetence, inefficiencies, speed, privacy, intermediaries, energy, and trust. It single-handedly improved upon existing financial infrastructure in nearly every way possible, and we're still just in the beginning stages when it comes to adoption.

Bitcoin

Bitcoin was created during the tail end of the great recession with some of the smartest people in computer science working out how to make a digital cash system. The timing here was key, as the very nature of bitcoin would not allow for the events that led to the 2008 recession to repeat themselves.

Bitcoin is the first and biggest cryptocurrency that uses cryptography to create a system that records transactions on the blockchain utilizing a proof of work mechanism. The proof of work mechanism is the form of proof in which one party proves to another that a specified amount of computational effort has been expended. Plainly, exchanging power (computational power that is) for bitcoin.

Like most money today, bitcoins are digital. There's nothing physical you can touch when owning a bitcoin. You can't cash it in and get a physical coin to put in your pocket. Much like your bank account statement, all that exists are rows of transactions and balances.

When you "own" any amount of Bitcoin, it means you own the right to access a specific Bitcoin address recorded in the ledger, and you can send funds from it to a different address. For the first time in the existence of digital money, everyone around the world now has an alternative to the current centralized system. No government or bank can control it.

Bitcoin offers a decentralized solution to money. Here are some reasons why it's gotten so popular so fast:

1. It gives you complete control over your money. You and you alone can access your funds with Bitcoin. A government or bank cannot confiscate your money.

2. It cuts out a lot of the middlemen from the process of transferring money. It's cheaper to use than traditional wire transfers or money orders. And unlike Fiat currencies, Bitcoin was designed to be digital by nature, which means you can add additional layers of programming on top of it and turn it into "Smart money."

3. It opens digital commerce to 2.5 billion people around the world who don't have access to the current banking system. Someone in a poor village of Africa can get into the cryptocurrency market as long as they are connected to the internet. They no longer get penalized because of where they live or whom they were born to. They can get involved in finance with the click of a button.

But if you think cryptocurrency has become mainstream, think again. The road to overall acceptance is still a long one. And that's great news for you! Because should you learn how to get involved in cryptocurrency now, the odds are very favorable in the long run.

Cryptocurrency is the wave of the future. In my personal opinion, and in those of highly respected investors, business tycoons, and many people in all parts of the world, it can't be stopped. No government or bank could if they wanted to. Over 70,000 computers around the world support the network running bitcoin software today. And it's still in its infancy!

The creation of bitcoin solved two major problems facing the digital world — double spending and counterfeiting.

The problem of double spending would arise in the digital world when trying to spend/send a digital currency twice. This effectively creates a disparity between the spending record and the amount of the currency available. For example, say I have a picture on my phone, and I sent that picture to two friends Jack and John. That picture now exists in three separate places – with me, with Jack, and with John. This scenario properly illustrates double spending in a way that doesn't cause a problem. The problem occurs when the "picture" is instead money. When I send digital currency to Jack, the ownership must also be stripped from me so that I cannot send the currency to John double spending it.

Counterfeiting is a concept that is much easier to understand and is simply the idea of attempting to falsify a digital file. If someone was to successfully falsify a bitcoin then the entirety of the bitcoin ecosystem would be rendered useless as the system would be corrupted.

The solution to both double spending and counterfeiting that bitcoin brought to life is called the blockchain.

Blockchain

The blockchain is a decentralized, distributed ledger that records the provenance of a digital asset. Put simply, the blockchain is a public record of transactions that utilizes certain technology that allows transparency, efficiency, and added security.

The way this works is that transactions are grouped together and included in a "block" of data that is then either confirmed and added to the blockchain or rejected and no longer presented to the public at all. The confirmation process enables immense security as the transaction must be confirmed by 51% of a distributed network.

With the decentralization of Bitcoin, unlike banks, there's not just one computer that holds the ledger. Every computer that participates in the system is also keeping a copy of the ledger, also known as the Blockchain. So, if anyone wanted to hack the ledger, he or she would have to take down tens of thousands or hundreds of thousands of computers which are not only keeping a copy of the ledger, but also constantly updating it.

Satoshi Nakamoto

Satoshi Nakamoto is the alias of the person or persons who created bitcoin, the original bitcoin whitepaper, and the implementation of the first blockchain. The legend of Satoshi Nakamoto is truly amazing as the identity has yet to be uncovered to this day. Not only has Nakamoto not been unveiled, but the initial mined coins that belong to Nakamoto have not moved since bitcoin's inception, all one million coins sit untouched in Nakamoto's wallets to this day.

Even though a large part of the crypto community believes that Nakamoto will never be unveiled there is a theory of who Nakamoto could be. In the early days of bitcoin there was an incredible computer scientist that worked alongside Satoshi Nakamoto within the early bitcoin developments by the name Hal Finney. Finney himself even developed the Proof of Work system that bitcoin uses today. And on January 11, 2009, the first bitcoin transaction ever was sent from Satoshi to Hal Finney. The theory goes that Satoshi Nakamoto and Hal Finney are the same person. Unfortunately, Finney passed away in 2014, and with him went all the secrets about bitcoin's birth.

The mysterious creator behind bitcoin is a point of strong contention within the community and will likely never come to an end. The anonymous creation of bitcoin allows for the true idea to shine over any potential attack that could come to an individual. One thing is for sure, no matter who the true creator of bitcoin is, their invention will certainly be one of the greatest technological innovations in history.

Smart Contracts

Smart contracts are programs on a blockchain that autonomously execute agreements. These contracts allow for increased efficacy because the program is carried out immediately, but only once the predetermined conditions are met. Real world use cases include faster banking transactions, a total replacement of escrow, entirely digitized identity management, and more. Current applications in the tangible world function through the use of a centralized server. This is the reality we are familiar with, but it is not as efficient as a Dapp. A Dapp, or a decentralized application, is a platform enabled by a blockchain. They allow users to interact with smart contracts that have deployed on the blockchain.

Altcoins

An altcoin is simply any cryptocurrency other than Bitcoin. As of the publication of this book there are over 8,000 altcoins in existence. I'd like to share a brief overview of some of the more notable project that exist and could very well prosper in the future.

Ethereum is the second largest coin and often people will talk about "the big two" in the realm of cryptocurrency referring to both Bitcoin and Ethereum. Ethereum refers to itself as "A technology that's home to digital money, global payments, and applications." Ethereum is most famous for the applications though. The Ethereum blockchain is different from the bitcoin blockchain because is supports smart contracts. People often argue that because Ethereum allows for the implementation of application beyond a cash system the potential growth is larger. Now is that statement true? That's for you to decide.

The next coin that I'd like to talk about had immense exponential growth in the last bull cycle and is called Binance Coin. Binance coin is the cryptocurrency issued by the largest cryptocurrency exchange—Binance. The coin is primarily used for trading and transaction fees when using Binance, but it has many other use cases. The coin can be used to make and process payments, buy virtual gifts, make loans, donate to charity, etc. Binance Coin is the leading coin in the category called exchange tokens, which are simply assets native to an exchange.

Tether, commonly referred to by its ticker symbol USDT, is the first and biggest stablecoin. A stablecoin is a cryptocurrency that, like most other coins, utilize a blockchain, cryptography, etc. But the differentiator is that USDT does not have any volatility. The price stays relatively stagnant at a 1:1 ratio between USD and USDT. This allows for individuals to transact using cryptocurrency and even utilize benefits such as staking or liquidity pools without any volatility.

The last altcoin I'd like to talk about is Cardano. This coin holds a special place in my heart as it was the first altcoin I ever seriously invested in back in 2017, and is a project that has not only generated great profits for me, but is one that I am truly passionate about. Cardano is a proof of stake blockchain platform, which is a characteristic that Ethereum also exemplifies. the scrutiny of others and all practices are designed to be based on scientific evidence.

But Cardano is "The first to be founded on peer-reviewed research and developed through evidence-based methods." This means that the work put into the project has been put under the scrutiny of others and all practices are designed to be based on scientific evidence.

As with all of these coins my goal is not to convince you to go and immediately buy them. I simply want to inform you of the alternative projects that exist beyond Bitcoin. I recommend you investigate many before investing in one. And always remember that there are 8,000 more coins waiting to be looked at.

NFTs

NFTs are the hottest new digital asset taking the world by storm as of 2021. NFT stands for Non-Fungible Token and is simply a unique digital asset. The cryptocurrencies that you are now familiar with, such as Bitcoin and Ethereum, have native assets that trade on the existing Bitcoin and Ethereum blockchains, however all the coins are the same. Jack's bitcoin is the exact same as John's bitcoin. An NFT on the other is hand, is completely unique. It cannot be replicated and is inherently a one-of-a-kind asset easily verifiable using the blockchain.

Some people still don't understand the purpose of an NFT and struggle to see how anyone should ever attribute any value to them. So, let me try to present an analogy to you. People like to collect things. Whether it's fine art straight from Sotheby's auction house, a rookie baseball card of your favorite player, an antique jeep driven in wartime, a ticket to the Broadway show you saw when you were a kid, I'm talking anything. We attribute value to these items and this value can be reflected by a widespread market, or by the personal value we attribute to it. All an NFT does is allow that same value, the value presented in the physical world, to be held digitally.

These NFTs are tokenized versions of art, collectibles, photos, videos, audio, or even real estate. When you own an NFT, you own all rights to that image. The virtual aspect allows for limitless application. Think about that upcoming sporting event of concert you've been wanting to go to. Now imagine if the ticket was an NFT. All aspects of the ticket buying process would be the same except you could buy and sell the tickets far more efficiently than the current systems in place. Furthermore, the ticket is permanently on the blockchain and can double as a collectible or resalable item after the event.

Web 3.0

The internet as we know it today is broken into three distinct times Web 1.0, Web 2.0, and now Web 3.0. These times all served their purpose, but it's important to understand the progression between the three.

In Web 1.0, from 1989-2005, the web was a place to obtain information. It was commonly known as the read-only web in which users were consumers of information with only businesses using it as a place to broadcast information to users who searched for it.

Later, from 2005-2020, Web 2.0 launched the era in which anyone could create and share information. Consider blogging, public forums, social media, YouTube videos, etc. The bland static webpages that existed previously had drastically improved allowing the user to interact with the page. Content creation could be done by anyone and everyone and a participatory culture began to take place.

Finally, in 2021 and onward, Web 3.0 aims to put control and ownership of content back into the hands of users. In Web 2.0 we made great progress creating an interactive experience with enhanced interoperability. Exponential growth was coupled with key innovation, but Apple, Microsoft, Facebook, and a select few other companies were the ones that benefited the most.

Web 3.0 is shaping up to be a paradigm shift even bigger than Web 2.0. The concepts of decentralization and enhancing user utility are driving the path to a more efficient digital future. To clarify, decentralization in terms of the internet allows for a permissionless system in which no centralized entity can act as a single point of failure; this further advances the idea of an internet free of surveillance and censorship. Furthermore, the infrastructure is a bottom-up system in which user input is prioritized which will maximize participation and experimentation.

Now I know that was a lot. Years and years of learning about cryptocurrency and I attempted to sum up all the necessary fundamentals in a single chapter. I urge you to reread this chapter if you are new to this world, because it is easy to gloss over some of the intricacies and never truly understand. Furthermore, I encourage you to pick a subheading and do some more research on it right now. Maybe NFTs are fascinating to you, but you're still a bit skeptical. I recommend exploring some existing NFTs on OpenSea—the number one NFT marketplace. Maybe you want to know more about the mysterious origin of Satoshi Nakamoto, you'll quickly discover that Hal Finney is not the only theory out there. Maybe a specific altcoin I talked about piqued your interest and you want to do a deep dive into the specifics to see if it would make a good investment. Who knows, maybe you'll even stumble across something that ends up changing your life.

CHAPTER 4
Qualities of a Good Investor

Savvy Investors

There are many great investors out there. Many of them make a ton of money. Some really smart ones however, don't. Investing isn't like baking a cake where you use the same ingredients over and over again to get the desired decadent chocolate cake. There is no recipe to follow that works every time. You don't do A, and B, in order to get to C. The results for the same actions taken on different investments yield different results- every time.

Successful investors/traders understand that accruing wealth through investments and trades is not a sprint, it's a marathon. Just as with everything that takes a long time, the first thing you need is patience. Had I not had patience to stick with baseball, even though every reasonable solution was for me to stop embarrassing myself and not sign up the following year, I wouldn't be where I am today. But, as my mother always said, "quitting is not an option". The same perseverance that I brought into my sport and music I brought into crypto as well. The best practice in investing is often to hold on to what you've purchased, no matter how bad it gets. I didn't make great profits my first three months. However, I kept going. Some of the kids I had talked to, tried their hand in cryptocurrency but after not seeing huge gains in the first 3-6 months, they gave up.

You will never win the investment game if quitting is an option. Although I had some decent, quite exciting wins early on, it took three years for my patience to be rewarded. Not only did I not quit, I also did the next best thing to become a good investor; I stayed informed.

As I sought to improve as an athlete, I didn't only go to the team practices, I also worked out individually, either by myself or with a trainer. I studied film, and became a student of the game. By the way, most of my studying came from YouTube videos. Inexplicably, there are people that shun YouTube videos to learn things. They would rather follow a professional or go to a conference or read books or pay for a course. All of that is good, but don't discount the vast amount of knowledge that is freely available on YouTube.

I watched hours and hours of YouTube videos. I siphoned out the bad advice from the people that knew what they were talking about rather quickly. I saved some great videos and watched them over and over and over again. As the saying goes, repetition works.

I wouldn't follow blindly to what the so-called experts were saying. I would follow their lead but then go and do my own research- reading whitepapers, analyzing competition, and looking into what the project was going to accomplish. I would compare their advice with my research and gauge it against my gut instincts and, if everything was in alignment, I would quickly pull the trigger. Although the first step is patience, when an investment is sound, hurry up and execute the trade. And that is the third quality of investing, having enough competency to produce results. What I'm saying in no way means you'll be right all of the time, but I can tell you from my personal experience that whenever the data supported an investment and I had a good feeling about it, it often worked out well for me.

All markets crash from time to time, it doesn't matter if it's a security, real estate property, commodity, or cryptocurrency. But, I want to stress the silver lining in losing money; sometimes, it's the best teacher. It sobers you up, it forces you to work harder, it's like getting a bucket of cold water poured over you – it refocuses you. Not to mention, it trims away all the people who don't belong in the market.

I once lost $39,874 in one day! I had not set up a Stop Loss on a transaction and thousands of dollars slipped away from my portfolio. (Could've been worse, at least it wasn't $40,000.) No matter what, you will have losses. You can be a prepared pitcher on the mound and throw a perfect pitch, but if the batter executes a perfect swing, it's not going to go your way...

So, if you're looking to make a list, here it is:

1. Have Patience
2. Increase Competency
3. Trust Your Instincts
4. Ignore the Short Term

Still Down 5 to 4

I calmly walked into the dugout, hoping we'd score two runs and win the game on the bottom of the sixth. I would have been a hero, having struck out their best hitter. However, we only scored one run and tied the game. Before I knew it, I was back on the pitcher's mound. The euphoric adrenaline wasn't as intense as when I faced a single batter. Now I had to retire the side without giving up any runs in order for us to have a chance to win. The sprint had turned into a marathon.

I got up, zoned in, and dealt. I got 3 straight outs, with one of them being a strike out. The place was pandemonium! I was no longer nervous. I was in the zone. As our team battled, I was relishing getting back on that mound and dealing again. I had waited too long, I'd been counted out for too long, I'd been called Easy Out and the worst player in my county, but I had stuck with it and I realized that the moment wasn't too big for me. I had put in years of sacrifice into honing my craft and had earned the right to be in that tumultuous position.

The game went into extra innings and I was out on the mound for the third time. Although I was still coated in sweat, so much so that my hat was falling off on every single pitch, I was zoned in. Even my cutter and curveball left my hand perfectly. I was ready to give the opponent my full arsenal of weaponry.

The game went into extra innings and I was out on the mound for the third time. Although I was still coated in sweat, so much so that my hat was falling off on every single pitch, I was zoned in. Even my cutter and curveball left my hand perfectly. I was ready to give the opponent my full arsenal of weaponry.

The first batter came up, and then walked back to the dugout.
The second batter came up, and then walked back to the dugout.
The third batter came up... and again walked back to the dugout with his head down.Once again I retired the side collecting 3 straight outs. My teammates, coaches, and the fans were still going crazy, but I stayed locked in.

In the bottom of the 8th inning, my teammate drove in the game winning run. I was finally able to celebrate the championship win and revel in the moment with my teammates. At the conclusion, I was awarded Player of the Week for the entire tournament, or at least, that's what the shirt they gave me said.

About thirty or forty minutes later, I announced to the team I had committed to play college baseball at the University of Tampa. The reaction was exactly how you'd envision it. All in all, that was a great day.

Winning Comes at a Cost

You don't win big without sacrificing anything. In sports, you might have to sacrifice hanging out with friends, a girlfriend, or hours of video games a day in order to train and build up your muscle memory. That's where honesty and integrity comes into play. For me, integrity is what you do when there is no one monitoring your decisions. Or, when you think no one is monitoring you.

You don't win big without sacrificing anything. In sports, you might have to sacrifice hanging out with friends, a girlfriend, or hours of video games a day in order to train and build up your muscle memory. That's where honesty and integrity comes into play. For me, integrity is what you do when there is no one monitoring your decisions. Or, when you think no one is monitoring you.

When people ask me for the "secret" to my success in crypto, first I tell them, there's no secret. There's no silver bullet. No straight path to success. You have to be patient, increase competency, trust your instincts, and ignore the short term. (If you're really paying attention, you'll notice those are the four steps listed above.) But, if I did have a secret formula, I would argue it would be hitting the genetic intelligence jackpot along with a basic endless pursuit for success.

My parents were a high-profile couple. Then, my father was gone. My mother, now a single mom of three, did not wallow in misery. She continued to go after the life she wanted for herself and continued to push us to go after the lives we wanted for ourselves.

I grew up watching my mother earn people's trust through hard work, determination, and honest dealings. Even though she may have never said these words to me when I was younger, I learned to, first and foremost, be honest with myself. I learned not to apologize for success that's been earned. I came to grips that I wanted to be wildly successful but, in order to do so, I had to put everything I had into it.

Today, many adults, (remember, I just graduated high school as I write this) believe what I tell them when it comes to cryptocurrency. Not solely because of my portfolio, but because they know the Shembekars (my family) operate with integrity and that we are honest people who care about the success of others. And although this may not have anything to do with the qualities of being a good investor, I believe that the free-market guides everything towards its destination. That's one of the intangibles that cannot be quantifiable, but still very powerful

Today, many adults, (remember, I just graduated high school as I write this) believe what I tell them when it comes to cryptocurrency. Not solely because of my portfolio, but because they know the Shembekars (my family) operate with integrity and that we are honest people who care about the success of others. And although this may not have anything to do with the qualities of being a good investor, I believe that the free-market guides everything towards its destination. That's one of the intangibles that cannot be quantifiable, but still very powerful.

So, one more time, the qualities you need to become a good investor?

1. Patience
2. Competency
3. Instincts
4. Ignore the Short Term

Oh, and when there's time ticking on a trade, and the ball is in your hand, zone in and throw the pitch!

CHAPTER 5
You Have to Want It

Just Get Started

Not too long ago, three high school freshmen reached out to me through a DM on Instagram. Each one wanted the same thing – help on how to make money through cryptocurrency. Mind you, they didn't want help learning about crypto, they wanted the shortcuts. I didn't have a ton of time for any of them, let alone three people individually. However, we went to the same school so I answered each one: I'd love to help. Call me tomorrow or in the next forty-eight hours and I'll help you out.

Not one of them called me. Mind you, they reached out to me, I answered their request in a favorable manner, and then they went silent. I never heard from two of the kids again. The last one reached out to me much after the 48 hours and said he was sorry for not getting back to me and that he was busy.

I don't understand that type of mentality. I'm going to school, trading, playing baseball, I'm in a few different school clubs, learning real estate, yet I offer you the time from me that you requested and you're busy? I don't understand the psyche of people that publically profess the desire to do something and then do nothing about it.

I write this for you because I don't want you to be like any of those kids. You're reading this because you want to make money through cryptocurrency, so take the information I've shared here and implement it. Remember that fortune follows the aggressor!

You can't hit a ball you don't swing at. You can't make a basket you don't shoot.

You can't win a race you don't run. You can't pass a test you don't take. And you can't make money with cryptocurrency without beginning your investment journey. It's glaringly obvious, and yet still people don't do it.

Goals don't fall into your lap. Some people daydream of becoming athletes but spend their time playing video games, eating potato chips, and quite simply not pursuing athletic endeavors. Goals don't just happen; you have to make them happen.

Everyone desires a better life somehow, some way, but they have no desire, no dedication, and no drive. I've spent hundreds of nights up until about 4 AM putting in the hours within the industry. When we sleep in America, the rest of the world begins to trade. It's not the best idea to always be asleep when huge markets become active. Your ambition must be your driving force.

Anyone can see that the best of the best, such as Michael Jordan, Tom Brady, Muhammad Ali, and others spent countless hours working on their trade. But they're not the only ones. You must ask yourself who you really want to be. You can be the best, you can be above average, you can be mediocre, etc. Whatever it is you choose to be, understand that that is ok! In reality, people who are above average are only classified that way because there is an existing backbone of society that is below them in comparison. Now, since you're reading this book, I'm going to assume that you are on the right side of the bell curve, but to advance your percentile regardless of where you stand currently is the hard part. What makes any professional successful- athlete, investor, etc- is their ability to progress efficiently from their initial starting point. That's what it takes. The natural talent you are born with is irrelevant, if you don't go all in to maximize your potential, then you won't make it to the next level. People's stories may vary in circumstance, but it all boils down to the same innate desire. You have to want it.

If you're looking for this book to give you the magic potion for success, give it to someone with a more realistic mindset. I didn't go from $20 to a million dollars by playing video games. I studied. I took notes. I stayed up late. I compared trends. I read articles. I watched YouTube videos. I talked about it to anyone who would listen to me. Why? Because I have bigger goals that in the years to come won't fulfill themselves.

Courses are fine for some things. I can't personally recommend any crypto course because I've never taken one. My advice is this: instead of spending money on courses, obtain as much free information as you can first. The information you'll find on these free websites provides a near endless stream of information that is deep, factual, and relevant.

You want to invest in crypto? Awesome.
You need goals. Set up action items that will get you to what you define as success. You won't get to a place you've never been to without using a GPS. Sure, you might get lucky and reach your destination by wandering blind, but how much easier would it be to first know where you're going, and then create a roadmap to get there?

Accountability is Key

If you're in a team sport, it's easy to be held responsible by others, such as your coaches, teammates, fans, and even the equipment manager. You work out with the team so they see when you slack, and when you put in one hundred percent. When you're bench-pressing your fourth set and you're struggling, you have a spotter encouraging you and maybe others that shout their support. However, when you work out alone, it's totally different. You need an entirely different mindset.

If you're at a gym by yourself, no one is there to push you on that third set. No one will notice if you don't follow through for your fourth and last set. If you've planned to run five miles alone, no one is there to tell you to keep going when you turn back at the two-mile mark and walk the two miles back to your house. In order to successfully work out alone, the goal that's driving you has to be stronger than the pain you're putting your body through.

In terms of crypto, all I did was study the concept for roughly 2-4 hours every single day. No one puts a timer to my research, and no one calls me out if I don't study at all, but the reason the learning is effective is because no one has to. My goals keep me accountable. My word keeps me accountable. Honesty and integrity keep me accountable to myself so that I can evolve into a better investor every single day.

I started playing piano when I was five years old. My younger brothers Preston and Colin did as well. An instructor would come in and teach us all once a week for an hour at a time. Then, she would leave. The other 6 days and 23 hours were up to us. We would either practice and get better, or not practice and not improve. I was the oldest and a little more advanced, so the instructor naturally gave me a little more time. As a result, I became a slightly better piano player than my brothers. But, as my focus shifted from piano to cryptocurrency, and Preston's focus continued, his dexterity surpassed me quickly.

Today, Preston can play some of the most difficult concertos on the piano, and he's still in high school. If you don't know much about piano, the following may not impress you, but let me tell you that these are incredibly difficult to play, and Preston plays them well; Liebestraum No. 3, Rachmaninoff's Prelude in C# Minor, Debussy's Claire de Lune, Debussy's Arabesque, Chopin's Ballad No. 1 in G-Minor, and more to come. I've committed to the University of Tampa to play baseball, and yet Colin, with proper motivation, has the potential to excel beyond me.

I didn't write that to brag about my brothers. I wrote that as an example of what it takes to reach your goals. It takes hard work, sacrifice, balance, and intelligence.

Our mother has been teaching us these lessons our entire life.

If you ever met me in real life, you'll see that I'm humble at heart, so when you read the following sentences, know that I'm not trying to impress, but that I'm trying to impress upon you the need to take action. My four years in high school I was consumed by crypto, trained hours a day for baseball, learned real estate, aced all my classes at a high-achieving high school, was a 4-year member of the orchestra, and later received the notable as Most Likely to Succeed.

My point? If you want to become successful at crypto, you can't just talk about it. You have to want it. It won't come easy, and your resolve will be tested. However, if you study enough, and if you research enough, you will eventually see an opening. All you have to do is seize the opportunity when it presents itself and hold on for dear life.

Life is all about experiences. I don't see baseball or crypto as work, although I certainly put in a lot of time into both. I love to work out. I sacrifice my time and choose to put my body through agony, and I enjoy it. Why? Because it advances my game on the field allowing me to compete and most importantly- win. Similarly, I love to watch and study the landscape of the crypto world.

You must understand that the boring part of anything that happens behind the scenes is the most vital step in success. If you're an actress trying to make it in L.A., the steps to success don't occur during auditions, but beforehand when rehearsing scenes. If you're a poker player, the steps to success don't occur at the table, but rather at home memorizing the statistical advantages between every single hand.

To be good at anything, you need to fall in love with practice. Fall in love with reading and finding out about the different coins and opportunities in cryptocurrency. Chances are you're reading this because you want to make a ton of money in cryptocurrency, and the reality is, you can. I must challenge you though – if you can't sit down and at least read the 9-page bitcoin whitepaper that lays the foundation for cryptocurrency, how serious can you be?

In baseball, my tool as a pitcher was the ball, my tool as a hitter was the bat. In cryptocurrency, your tool is the wealth of information that is freely available at your disposal. If you don't practice, don't expect to play well. And if you don't fully analyze your investments, trying to pick them apart playing devil's advocate from every angle possible, don't expect them to be fruitful.

The world is full of mediocre people. It really isn't that hard to stand out of the crowd of humanity because billions of people have no idea what they want, and for those that do, most don't have the mindset to go after it. If you are driven, goal-oriented, integral, and resolute, you can be successful at whatever you put your mind to, including crypto.

CHAPTER 6
The Stock Market vs. Cryptocurrency

Saving vs. Investing

Before we get into this debate, let's first agree that one of the best ways to build wealth over time is through investing, not saving. Saving is different than investing. Saving money in your bank will grow your money very slowly, if at all. Saving your money in an IRA will grow your money over time. However, investing in the right real estate, stock, or cryptocurrency will grow your money substantially faster than by saving it in a bank account or IRA.

The NASDAQ, created by the National Association of Securities Dealer officially known as the FINRA (Financial Industry Regulatory Authority), has been around all my life. It was founded on February 8, 1971 and was created so that investors could trade securities on a computerized, speedy, and transparent system. It was the world's first electronic exchange. Most of the world's industry giants, including Apple, Microsoft, and Facebook, are listed on the NASDAQ and their shares can be bought or sold there.

It has been a vital economic accelerator for many people. It has allowed people who would never have had the ability to create much wealth turn into millionaires simply by choosing the right stocks (companies) to purchase. Conversely, it has been the demise of many peoples' financial dreams, as frauds, cheats, and scam artists have taken advantage of the naïve and gullible for years. Still, it is the most trusted entity for trading in today's global economy. Like everything great, competition exists, and the emerging industry of decentralized finance coupled with cryptocurrencies will begin to increase in prominence.

What Do You Mean You're Closed?

Banking and getting access to your cold hard cash often depends on someone else's schedule. Every bank opens and closes at a specified time. Perhaps you can recollect a time or two when you were in your car going as fast as you thought you could get away with to make it to your bank before it closed for the day. It's quite likely that if you did make it in time, you found yourself waiting in line for the teller or waiting to speak with someone in their wall-less office.

Similarly, the stock market has a daily start and end date. Traditionally, the markets are open from 9:30 AM – 4 PM Mondays – Fridays (normal business days). They are closed on weekends. To be more correct, you can make a trade or buy or sell a stock over the weekend and it will be put into a queue to be processed when the markets open on the next trading day, which is usually that Monday.

The problem with that is, nowadays, we are a *fast food, give it to me now, I hate waiting, I'll just valet the car instead of hunting for a parking spot*, civilization. It's almost as if our patience has dissipated. Even our grandparents seem to have the *why am I waiting* mindset nowadays.

Unlike the stock market and traditional banking, cryptocurrency doesn't close. The instant gratification that our society craves is tailor-made for a market that's ready to trade, buy, or sell, whenever they want; early morning, late at night, during weekends, and even on Christmas and New Years. The unlimited access to cryptocurrency is incredibly enticing and it's one of the reasons for its rapid growth.

Cryptocurrency is still in its infancy. Yet, if you're in the financial industry or into investing, you can't get away from it. It is constantly featured on financial-based television shows on powerhouse networks, such as CNBC and FOX. I've spoken to retired people of over 80 years of age about cryptocurrency with the same amount of enthusiasm and optimism as with 17-year-olds. Cryptocurrency transcends all age groups and is here to stay.

3 Fun Facts:

1. Stocks have been around for centuries, while cryptocurrency has only been around since 2008 with its inception occuring during the financial crisis.

2. When you buy a share of stock, you hold onto it in the hopes that it continues to grow and become more profitable. When you buy tokens of a particular currency, just as with a stock, you also hold onto the tokens in the hopes that they will increase in value. The differentiator here is that, depending on the token or coin, you can also use them as a form of payment. You can't do that with a stock.

3. You don't buy crypto the way you buy stocks. To buy stock into a company, you trade on the traditional stock exchange. With crypto, most people use a crypto exchange – a website – and you store them in your digital wallet.

Both markets can be very volatile. That means to buckle up and hold on for a wild ride because you can be in store for big wins and big losses. As I write this, Ethereum has been down by around 35% in the last two weeks. So, if you bought Ethereum in the last couple of weeks, it looks like you've lost your money. But hold on to it and I'll tell you why.

Over the past year, Ethereum has seen its price increase by 1,200%! And that includes the major downturn the last couple of weeks. On the flip side, the S&P

500 is only up 42%. Meaning, in January of 2021 if you invested in the S&P 500, you've made an increase of up to 42% - and that's great. However, if, in January of 2021, you invested in Ethereum, you would've made in increase of 1,200%. Which would you have rather invested in?

The diagram below from The Motley Fool depicts it best:

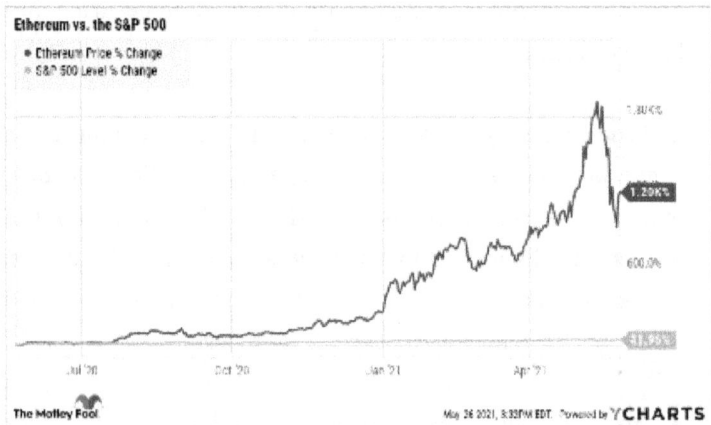

If you believe "Slow and steady wins the race" then, by all means, invest in the S&P 500. But if, like me, you're looking for bigger returns and can handle not being risk-averse then cryptocurrency may be for you.

The Digital Wallet

Many people overthink what a digital wallet is and their confusion scares them away for investing in cryptocurrency. So, let me explain what it means. It's a wallet, much like you have in your pocket or purse. Your physical wallet holds your license, debit card, credit card, cash, maybe your insurance cards, and maybe even a business card of someone you intend to reach out to. Either way, you get my point. You know what your wallet is.

A digital wallet is the same thing but electronic. To be more specific, a cryptocurrency wallet is a software or hardware application that allows cryptocurrency users to store and retrieve their digital assets, much as you would store and retrieve assets from your physical wallet.

The difference with having access to your physical wallet than with your digital wallet is that you can just reach into your pocket and grab your wallet. Conversely, someone who isn't you (a thief!) can also reach into your pocket and grab your wallet. A digital wallet, which holds your information much like a physical wallet, is similar to a safe. Meaning, that if you don't have the code or keys to get into the safe, you can't get into the wallet. A digital wallet is protected by a unique set of "keys."

Public Keys and Private Keys

There is a public key and a private key for every digital wallet. Consider your public key much like you do your email address. It's not a secret. And, unless you want to protect it from spammers, you don't mind people knowing your email address. Just by knowing your email address they can't gain access to your emails and the sensitive information on some emails. In crypto, a public key is used for people to send and encrypt messages for a particular recipient.

A private key is like the password to your email. Just like a password, a private key is nothing but a string of numbers and letters.

Here's where it gets tricky but that's okay, if it doesn't become clear the first time you read the next couple of paragraphs, simply read them again and I assure you, you'll get it.

If you're on a centralized exchange, the exchange is the custodian of your private key. Much like when you put your money in an IRA, you trust the custodians of the IRA. Similarly, crypto users put their trust in the exchange and leave their coins in the exchange, just as someone "leaves" their money in an IRA.

A centralized exchange is in essence, a website (a middleman) that promotes and holds lots of coins for distribution. There is an entity or a group that governs it. The biggest and most trusted centralized exchanges are Binance and Coinbase. Basically, those sites or apps let you use their software product to make it easier for you to securely store, send, and receive different tokens.

If you don't use a centralized exchange, that means no entity is in possession of your private keys. You, the consumer, are the only one that has access to your private keys. This means that you have added security as well as added responsibility.

I told you, you'd get it!

In closing, while the Stock Market and the Crypto Market may seem similar, the latter presents entirely new opportunities that the Stock Market cannot offer with the new implementation of technology such as blockchain, decentralization, and a market that does not sleep.

CHAPTER 7

The Pool Table, The Map, and The Pins

Life Isn't Fair

Sometimes, you're going to go through things that, even as traumatic as it might be, will make you a better person, or will take you to places you never thought you would get to. Parents who sadly lost a child to a drunk driver make it their mission to spread the word and fight against drunk drivers. People who lose a loved one to cancer donate part of their life's savings to finding a cure so that others don't go through the same thing.

Pain or embarrassment often provokes glory. The pain of hunger, of not having enough, of extreme poverty, of being ridiculed and made fun of have often been the springboard to people digging deep inside of themselves and becoming wildly successful, whether it be in the literary world, sports, music, business, real estate; you name it.

No one goes through life without serious disappointments or heartbreak. For me, it happened when I was eight years old.

My life, to that point, had been great. I didn't know it at the time, because a kid's perspective of the world is mainly from home, but we were very well off financially. We lived in a big mansion, had nice cars, and traveled to really cool destinations. Again, I didn't know how good we had it because I didn't know enough people to compare our standard of living with. All I knew was my mom was awesome, my dad traveled a lot and was cool, and, as the oldest of three boys, I had a little bit of influence in the games we played and the activities we participated in.

The Single Mother

My father was, based on my mother's memories, a rock solid person. They had been successful individually, but when they got married, they became a power couple in the area, especially within the Indian community. They were business savvy philanthropic entrepreneurs and were even active in helping others succeed.

The problem was that my father was always absent. He was constantly traveling on business. There are parents in the military that saw their children more than my father saw us. The worst part about that is that he didn't need to do all of that traveling. Money was not an issue. My father traveled about 28 days out of a month simply because he wanted to. It was as if he was addicted to going from one stop to another.

To his credit when he would come home, he'd take some time to play cards with me and taught me how to play pool. But that's because that's what he wanted to do, not what I wanted to do. With my younger brother Preston, he would take him flying. Mom says that Preston would cry, "I don't want to go flying!" What six or seven year old boy wants to spend hot, Tampa days on a tarmac prepping a plane and doing pre-flight checks? Not Preston!

Still, we craved his attention. I would hardly be able to sleep the nights before I knew he was coming to visit. But that's what it was, a visit. He wasn't coming home; he was coming for a visit. That was my dad.

Time continued to tick by and a rift in the marriage began to develop. And with his continued absence, the rift widened and they both decided to part ways.

I can barely remember this memory, and yet I'll never forget it. I was eight-years-old, Preston was seven, and Colin was four. We were sitting on the staircase by the front door in the evening with dim lights. My father asked my mother to wait outside while he talked to us briefly. As he came back inside, he locked the glass doors behind him.

My mother could see everything, patiently waiting outside as he began what we remember as his infamous speech. He huddled us all together and began to say "I'm leaving and never coming back. You will never see me again." ... I let out a horrific shriek experiencing what I can only describe as the strongest negative emotion I had ever felt. My brothers begin to follow suit screaming and crying and my mother begins to pound on the door only adding to the flow of emotion.

How does a boy respond to something like that? Writing this now as a young adult I'm still dumbfounded. Badly I guess. I cried all night. My mother came to my room because I was hyperventilating. Dad was leaving but this time he was never coming back. An atomic bomb had gone off in my little world and changed it forever.

My father is many things, one of them being, he's true to his word. He never came back. My brother's and I never got a phone call, no "Happy Birthdays.", no Christmas cards, nothing. After that, a single mom raised us.

There are many books, backed by real statistics, that talk about how much more difficult it is for children raised by a single mother to become successful. In fact, a report on Crime and Justice via heritage.org says that the real root cause of violent crime comes from the breakdown of families and marriages. High-crime neighborhoods are characterized by high concentrations of families abandoned by fathers. Conversely, 90% of children from safe, stable homes do not become delinquents.

The good news for us was that our mother was not your run-of-the-mill, woe-is-me, single mother. The fact that her husband wanted out of the marriage did not in any way change the futures she wanted for herself and her boys. Being that "dad" was hardly there anyway, our normal, every day world didn't actually change that much. The only difference really was that mom made sure to spend lots and lots of time with us.

As a family, we still took lots of great trips. Mom worked on puzzles with us, read to us, taught us how to swim and ski... she was always present. Many people would tease her during my baseball practices because although she never missed one, she was almost always on the phone.

But my father was cunning. He convinced my mother to sign the mansion over to him before the divorce was finalized. So, when they divorced, he told her that we had 30 days to vacate our home, or he would call the sheriff's office and they would escort us out. Within 30 days, I left the only home I had known.

- I'd like to add a side note to this part of our story. My mother ended up buying back the mansion from my dad. When he asked her why he should sell it to her, even though she had bought it the first time, she said, "Three reasons: Jackson, Preston, and Colin."

As I got older, I of course made friends with other kids whose parents were divorced, but it was always different than our scenario. Their father's would see them on weekends; some had shared custody, and even those whose father's moved away, they kept in touch with their children. Not our dad. We got the pleasure of being part of a highly elite 1% club in which our father chose a high-flying lifestyle over his own children.

Yet, our mother never let us feel less than because we didn't have a father. Actually, she kept us too busy to even notice most of the time. School, homework, piano, basketball, baseball, etc. – then I got into crypto – we didn't miss a beat. We all got straight A's in school, and we all excelled in music and in sports. Again, this is not to brag on my brothers, or myself, it's to brag on my mom.

The Blue Pin

I was a sophomore in high school and there was a school-wide creative writing competition. We all had to write an essay based on a bunch of ideas the teachers put into a scrapbook. There was a page in the scrapbook that had a bunch of planes in it. Instantly, I knew what I was going to write about. My intuition was telling me that I could win the whole thing!

I wrote the essay and won the contest! My prize: to read it in front of the whole school. As you might expect, I was nervous. All of the students were going to be there, as well as the teachers, coaches, priests, and many parents, including my mother. I learned something about nerves though, they aren't nearly as debilitating as long as you prepare. I read my essay over and over again, I printed it out, I double spaced, and I even marked in there the times I would look up from the page. When I read it, I had a finger under every word so that when I looked up, I wouldn't lose my place after looking into the faces of more than 1,200 people.

This is what I wrote:

The Pool Table, the Map, and the Pins

My dad was a great guy. He came to America from India when he was a kid, along with my grandparents. He worked hard in school: learning the English language, becoming top of his class, and even playing basketball and football throughout college. He also met my mom in college, and they both continued on to be very successful. They both traveled the world and pursued public speaking, which in turn requires lots of time and energy.

Soon later, my mom had her first baby–me. She wanted to be there for me, so she decided to give up everything to raise me, and let my dad continue to travel and provide for our family. As I got older, I began to understand all of the great sacrifices he made being away from his family. Therefore, a tradition was born.

Whenever he would come home from his business trips we would play a game of pool, and to the right of the pool table was a map. The map was filled with red pins. Each red pin represented a place he had traveled to, and there was one blue pin. This was a special pin because it represented the next destination he was headed to for work. So whenever he would come home we would play a game of pool, place a red pin on the map, and move the blue pin to a new location. As a kid this was amazing to me, the map began to fill up with red pins and I knew where every single one was, all 178 of them.

One day, my dad came home from a trip to Paris. He was gone for two weeks and I was thrilled to see him. When he walked in the door, I gave him a hug and we began to walk upstairs to start our habitual game of pool. After 10 minutes, I lost like usual and we approached the map.

We grabbed a red pin and together, pressed it into the center of Paris, and moved the blue pin that used to be there to Dubai- the next location. Even after pressing in those pins 179 times it never got old, the simple action of pressing a red pin into the map represented the unbreakable bond that I will always have with my dad.

Later that night, my parents asked me if they could talk to me about something serious. I was only eight years old at the time, and nothing could prepare me for the words I was about to hear that night. They both said in unison, "Jackson, we are getting a divorce."

My heart sunk, and as an eight year old I didn't fully understand what those words meant, but I knew they weren't good. Little did I know that my unbreakable bond with my dad was shattered in that moment.... Now, seven years later, I have forgotten how to play pool, and there are still 179 pins on the map, with a special blue pin on Dubai.

I ended to a thunderous applause. Later, parents, teachers, students, and coaches all told me how they didn't know the gravity of my situation. I got tons of congratulations, and some even told me that my speech moved them so much, they cried. It was at that moment that I realized I enjoyed public speaking and that I can have an impact on an audience.

What This Means for You

Life is going to come at you hard. Life isn't going to play fair. It surely didn't for my brothers or me. Raising three boys by herself is not what my mother envisioned when she married. I share the intimate story of being abandoned by a "good guy" to remind you that when you get knocked down, you have two choices, you can stay down and give up, or you can get back up.

In relation to trading or investing, there are times when you feel you've got it all figured out. Then, out of the blue everything can go wrong. Maybe you thought something was a good long-term investment, but in a matter of a few hours, it goes down by 20%.

Here's my advice. If the price goes down on something that you've researched, and there is nothing fundamentally different about the coin, project, company, etc. Double down and buy more!

Competent investors make up their minds prior to the purchase of a stock or coin. They are willing to ride out any potential future dips prior to investing. Of course, this logic only applies to you assuming that you are a competent investor. And of course, I'm going to assume you are one since you read Chapter 4.

When my dad left, I didn't know the term, but I was at rock bottom. I didn't stay there though. Neither did Preston nor Colin. Our mother made sure of it. Our mother invested in us. She left her career to be a mother. And, when things got worse and her husband left, she double-downed on us. The same philosophy applies to your investments.

When you start to lose money on a trade, don't give up on it. As people run for the hills in panic, buy while the price is low. When it goes up again you will find out that what you thought was going to break you is the thing that strengthens you.

CHAPTER 8

Emotion vs. Logic

Be Batman

Trading is... volatile. Regardless if you're trading stocks or crypto, there's no guarantee you'll end up making money. If there was a guarantee about trading it's this – once you trade long enough, there will be times when you lose money. When you lose, that doesn't mean to take out all of your money and stuff it in the mattress. Like Thomas Wayne said to a young Bruce Wayne, "Why do you fall? So you can learn to get up." Bruce went on to become Batman.

The problem with many crypto investors I know, whom I humorously refer to as degenerate millennials, is that they lack order and structure and rely on luck and feeling. They're the first ones to run for the hills, abandoning all reason, saying that crypto is a scam, only to come back later to try their luck like a roulette wheel.

If luck is the lynchpin of your investment strategy, you'd be better off filling up a sack with all your money, inserting a dumbbell into said sack, and swiftly disposing of the sack in the Atlantic Ocean. I don't rely on luck, although at times I've certainly benefited from it. For me, I use preparedness (research and studying the market) and opportunity (wait for what I'd like to see happen), followed by the boldness to execute (not overthink it and trust my research and make the trade), controlled by patience (riding it out with logic, not emotion), with a sprinkle of luck. That, my friend, is the winning formula. I'll never forget when I abandoned this formula. It was the biggest loss of my life.

By 2019, I had gone from $20 to about 100K, which was pretty cool for a kid just fiddling on a computer. I had invested in bitcoin and several other projects and was gradually making gains. Then, without warning or without me reading that the price had changed, the price started going up – fast.

The price hadn't gone back to double digit thousands since the bull cycle of 2017. It would fluctuate from around $6K to $8K. On this particular day, it started to shoot up: $8.2K, $8.5K, and $9K! Then it hit the double digit thousands and reached $11K!

As it was going up, I was freaking out. I thought I was going to make so much money! It was hard not to daydream about what I was going to do with all the winnings. Then, just as quickly as it started to go up, it starts to go down again. I was watching it more intently than I would watch a Game 7 of the World Series. I knew this was one of those flash opportunities of immense volatility where someone could win or lose drastically.

When it dropped down to $9K, I made my exit – I sold. I figured it would go back down to around $7K and I'd save a great amount of money on the way down. Right when I sold, however, it jumped to $9.5K, then back to $9.9K. Every time it went higher I saw money slipping through my fingers. Then, it started dropping again and got back to $9K. I was right. For about 2 minutes. But then, within five minutes the price shot up to $13K. I made a buy order and bought everything back, but now that it was a higher price, I didn't get nearly as much for my money.

You may not have followed all of that, and you don't need to. Just understand that at the end of the day, I lost a lot of bitcoin. To put that in perspective, I had a $200K portfolio at the time, and then lost approximately 20% of it. In real money, in a matter of minutes, I lost $39,874. Abiding by the principles encompassed in this book, that $39,874 would be worth upwards of $300,000.

Blood in the Streets

Warren Buffet is known as the Oracle of Omaha. He is currently listed as the sixth richest member of the Forbes 400 with a net worth of $108 billion as of May 2021. When Mr. Buffet talks, I listen. When Mr. Buffet gets interviewed, I watch. When Mr. Buffet writes an article, I read it. He says, "Buy when there's blood in the streets, even if the blood is your own."

I think of that often when I trade. The problem that day was that my emotions got the best of me. I sold when I shouldn't have and bought when I shouldn't have. I learned two very valuable lessons that day:

1. Don't trust your emotions
2. Sometimes, all you need is a break

Investing is a long game. When a volatile market starts to dance, trust your research and investment principles and go to the gym, take a run, or watch a movie. For me, when I lost $39,874 in a day, I walked into a Panda Express and got some food. My mind was still spinning. My heart was doing jumping jacks.

But I had to step back and let my logic take over. Instead, I enjoyed my orange chicken- which is clearly the logical decision as it is without a doubt the best item on the menu.

The biggest emotional times happen with there's a lot of volatility. The saying, "If you can't stand the heat, get out of the kitchen" is very relevant for traders. I made a market buy, thinking I was going to make thousands in mere minutes, the price shot down, and instead I lost thousands in seconds.

The Markets Want You to Win

There are three ways to put in a trade, each of which are designed to make it easier for you to win. These three ways are a Limit Order, a Market Order, and a Stop Loss.

- Limit Order: (It's also referred to as a Maker Order, because you make the order). Basically, this means you put a limit on the trade/ investment you want to make. For example, if Microsoft is trading at $250 but you don't want to buy it until it drops to $230, you put in a Limit Buy Order at $230. The trade is made in the books, but it will not execute unless the price of Microsoft drops to $230.

  Let's say it dropped and you bought it for $230. Now, you can put a Limit Sell Order at $300. So, if it rises back to its original $250, you keep it and have made money, and if it goes up to $300, you sell it. Now, you no longer own it, but you've made more money.

- Market Order: (Also referred to as a Taker Order) Essentially, this means you're buying in real time at whatever price the market dictates. If Microsoft is at $250, you're buying at that price, unlike buying when it drops to $230 with a Limit Order.

- Stop Loss: This is a little more advanced in execution, but still very easy to understand. Let's say you own shares of Microsoft at $250, but you think recent news may shift the price lower. So, you can place a Stop Loss at $200. That means that if the price goes under $200, it sells effectively halting any further losses.

The day I lost the $39,874 was because I had always done limit orders with set stop losses that would abide by my trading plan, but when the market became very volatile, I panicked and made a string of market orders. Pure emotions ruled that day and I struck out. Plain and simple.

Some people have told me that I learned a $39,874 lesson that day. I see the logic in that, because ever since then, when I get emotional about a trade, I go to Panda Express and trust my research. However, I don't see it as a $39,874 lesson in that I lost that amount. The way I see it, because I lost such a great amount that day, it had a significant impact on me. The mistake of not trusting my research and making an impulse decision helped change my identity as an investor and in the long run, helped mold me into a successful, and much more profitable investor.

Let me compare trading to war. You have to understand this very important truth about war; even the victors suffer losses. Losing battles is a part of war. If you can learn why you lost, your men and money will be safer the next battle because you will have drawn up a better battle plan.

Be self-critical. Be okay with not winning every day. Learn from your mistakes, believe me there will be plenty. And most importantly, when your emotions get the best of you, go to Panda Express.

CHAPTER 9
Marketology

Bulls and Bears

If you've ever been to New York City and you stood on Broadway, just north of Bowling Green, in the financial district of Manhattan, you've most likely seen one of the most famous statues in the United States. It's a 7,100-pound bronze sculpture that stands 11 feet tall and 16 feet wide. The statue is, of course, the Bull. Although there are many other statues in and around the Financial District, none symbolize Wall Street quite like the Bull. Everyone loves it when the Bull charges. Let me explain why.

Regardless of whether you invest in crypto, stocks, real estate, or any other asset, the markets are often described one of two ways; it's either a Bull Market or a Bear Market.

A bull market – or bull run – is when the market heats up. During this time, investors buy more, demand outweighs supply, market confidence is high, and prices rise. Everyone loves a good bull run because everyone is winning. When a stock or coin reaches the highest point, everyone who invested bought it at a lower price, so every single investor made money. It shouldn't come as a surprise that when they picked a color to represent the bull market, they chose green.

Bitcoin enjoyed a bull market in the last six months of 2020. Prices ranged from $5K to about $15K for three years prior, but in 2020 and 2021, it shot up from single-digit thousands all the way up to over $60K! If you had invested in Bitcoin, quite literally at any point, and held on to your investment, you would have made yourself a tremendous amount of money. Even more impressive is that other coins such as Binance Coin and Ethereum have had even bigger jumps! Not too long ago, the coin Cardano was at five cents; it's over a dollar as of this writing and I believe that it's still just the beginning.

A bear market is exactly the opposite. It's the term to describe when the market is down. Supply is greater than demand, confidence is low, and prices are falling. All of the excitement of the bull run has evaporated, and most people – panic sellers – think they need to sell before they start to lose money or before they lose more money than they've already lost.

Crypto experienced a bear market in 2018. The year prior, crypto went mainstream and experienced a massive uptick of investors. Before that, it wasn't taken too seriously by the overall financial industry, but now that people were made aware of the general notion of cryptocurrency, a news anchor was talking about it on CNBC every single day. It was almost as if every show looked outdated if they didn't interview a new "crypto expert."

And they talked about it for good reason; before 2017, Bitcoin was trading/ selling in the hundreds. Then it spiked, spiked again, and again, and again. People started making astronomical gains as it climbed all the way up to $20K.

Then, the bears showed up. First, it dipped a few thousand, and then almost everyone ran and headed for the hills, meaning a wave of panic-sellers figured to cut their losses and dump their coins. The result: Bitcoin lost 80% of its market cap (value of all bitcoin in existence). Imagine a once-thriving western town in the 1800s filled with competing saloons, busy stables, and new stores, compared to a barren town with the wind blowing tumbleweeds down an empty street a year later. The only people that kept Bitcoin alive were those that held on. When you buy and hold, people refer to you as a HODLer.

The word "hold." was once misspelled on a forum. The person spelled it "hodl." Instead of just shrugging off that one-time typo, the crypto community embraced it. Since then, the term HODL has been coined as "Hold On for Dear Life." The phrase expresses the wild volatility that comes with being a part of this brand-new market.

From 2018 to 2020, after the bear market, we saw a period of consolidation. I write this lightly as the volatility was still extremely high in comparison to nearly any other asset class. The price was static in the $6,000 to $10,000 range with brief periods above and below the extremes. Excluding the summer of 2019, nothing "exciting" was happening in the crypto world.

For a seasoned, patient investor, this was a great time to reassess. We now had years of data to analyze with mainstream attention. Cryptocurrency was not a secret anymore; the media and news outlets took care of that. Many people had lost a lot and many people had gained a lot. Of course, you're reading this to be the latter. So, you'll need to understand the psychotic psychology of a winning investor.

The Mindset of a Winning Investor

We live in a time where information is at our fingertips. Whatever you want to do, you can learn to do it. You can google everything and find many credible websites on how to do just about anything. If you think there is nothing out there pertaining to something you want to learn about, you simply haven't looked hard enough.

While all of that is great, the term mentor and apprenticeship has dwindled. Today, people of all ages open businesses, sometimes on a whim. They see someone be successful at something and they open a similar business. It's the way of the world today. Sadly, because people rush into opening a business, 87% of businesses don't make it more than five years.

I say this to emphasize that regardless of whether you start your journey at 14, 64, or even 104 years-old you need someone that has been in your shoes to guide you on your road to success. Many of my mentors have no idea I follow them and write down what I hear them say or what I read from them. As I mentioned earlier, one of those mentors is the great Warren Buffet – primarily regarded as the greatest investor ever.

Market psychology is a complex battle between the mind and the charts. Everyone knows the famous rules for investing: "Buy Low, Sell High." Yet for some reason, it is so difficult to execute. The chart below sums it up best.

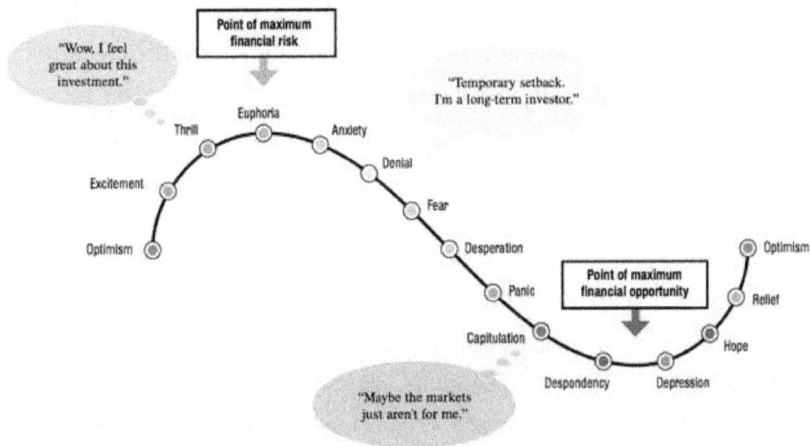

You need to be a contrarian investor. I'm not saying you should be, I'm not saying consider being - I'm saying that you NEED to be a contrarian investor. Meaning, don't follow the sheep, and instead watch what the shepherds are doing. When the bitcoin price was trading at $30,000, people were excited the price was at an all-time high and in price discovery mode. Then, Telsa announced it would accept Bitcoin as payment, and it shot to $40,000. Not shortly after, with additional institutional support in combination with healthy on-chain metrics, the price quickly rose to $60,000. That stage was clearly the

Euphoria - that's when things were at an all-time high and continuing to climb. Everyone was winning, and therefore nobody was losing. More people heard about it and started to buy. I stress this because if everyone is winning, the progression cannot be sustained for very long. Think about this, if your cousin's 93-year-old grandma is investing and she doesn't even have an email address, it may be time to worry.

Dumb Money is a term when inexperienced people flood money into the market. Greed takes over reasoning and "easy money investors" and "get-rich-quick investors" drive the prices very high. These are the ones that ultimately lose money and tell all their friends not to invest in cryptocurrency. They have played a large part in people not trusting cryptocurrency, but they're either too ignorant or too proud to admit it's their own fault. Hope, optimism, and greed are the driving forces of euphoria. You'll read this over and over in this book: don't invest with emotion; be pragmatic.

So your cousin's grandmother was happy. She got in with Bitcoin when it was at $50,000 and it shot up to $60,000. Who knows, maybe she was looking to buy a motorized walker, maybe even attach some neon lights. Then the price started to drop. It got to $45,000 then $40,000 and then $32,000. She most likely sold it, and it continued to go down to $30,000 and then $28,000. She felt like a true investor because she was smart enough to mitigate her losses. To her, in a sense, the extra $2,000 she could have lost is money that, in a way, she made. Ladies and gentlemen, that's how "experts" are made in the world of investing. People listen to those who know how to mitigate their losses over those who have made fortunes. It's baffling, really, but it's true.

My point is, when everyone is selling, my friend, it's the best time to buy. When you don't think it can get any lower, when all the rats have jumped off the Titanic, is when you need to buy. It makes more sense to buy when the prices are going up, but that will only make you cents on the dollar. The big wins come with the big risks. And that is why I say, *only invest what you can lose.*

The psychology of an investor sometimes mirrors psychosis. It makes no sense to hold on to your investment when half the people are cashing out or cutting their losses. I get it. However, when I invest in a new coin or infuse additional capital, I do it with psychosis psychology. Every fiber of my being tells me that it's foolish to "send good money after bad money." But then I reason to myself to do what the proven geniuses have done. My research and self-control predetermine my decisions.

You who are reading this, what I'm going to say to you may be hard to do, but when your investment starts to crash and burn, don't make a rash decision, do more research. If your research is sound, wipe the blood off your digital wallet and buy when there's blood in the streets, even if it's your own. The same volatility that scares tire-kickers away from investing in crypto is what can make you wealthier than you have ever dreamed. You must understand bull markets, bear markets, and psychology. If you can read the signs and understand to be pragmatic, eventually, you will win.

CHAPTER 10
Play Your Own Game

Cooperstown

If you're involved with youth baseball at a competitive level, chances are you've heard of Cooperstown Dreams Park. Right outside the city lies 22 baseball fields and 104 barracks where hundreds of teams come from across the nation to compete against the best of the best. It is known as the American Youth Baseball Hall of Fame, as it is located in Cooperstown, New York, home of the National Baseball Hall of Fame and Museum. The city is deeply intertwined within the fabric of baseball, so much so that if baseball were to be a person, Cooperstown would be the heart.

When I was twelve, I got invited to play in their annual tournament. It was like being invited to go to Disney World for baseball players. At the time, I was playing for the nationally recognized Coach Terry Rupp, and we had a great player/coach relationship. He liked me because he was old school and would not hesitate to yell at his players, and that didn't bother me at all. I loved the constructive criticism and the challenge, even if it was at decibels most kids wilted under. Unbeknownst to me, Coach Sal Urso, a former professional baseball player himself, had seen me pitch a no hitter with Coach Rupp's team. He brought a team to Cooperstown every year and asked Coach Rupp if I could join him to play with his team for the summer.

Coach Rupp, even though he was not afraid to get in anyone's face, was also very protective and possessive of me. He had a conversation with my mother and me and said, "People are going to come at you from all directions asking you to pitch. You've earned that. But that doesn't mean you should play for just anyone." He then turned to my mother and told her, "With that said, this is a once in a lifetime experience for Jackson that he can't pass up. Sal knows what he's doing. You should go for it."

When I went to practice with Coach Sal's team, I was a little nervous. Not so much of my pitching abilities, though; at the time I was already competing against an elite level of 12-year-olds. (I understand that sounds like an oxymoron but bear with me.) My reservations were more about fitting in. I learned early on that Coach Sal plays to win. He ran the team like a drill sergeant; he executed everything like clockwork, smoothly and efficiently.

That being said, Coach Sal didn't have much patience for people who committed errors. This was the first time his son was on his team, and others told me it was obvious that he had never wanted to win the Cooperstown tournament nearly as much as he wanted to win that year. I would later witness the firm command he had over his team. On one particular play, his son, the third baseman, was running full speed, eyes up, chasing down a foul ball, about to crash into a metal fence. Coach Sal yelled, "Slide!" and almost simultaneously, his command was processed, and the player slid safely while catching the ball. That's the type of team he ran. That's the type of players he had.

If you made a mistake on Coach Rupp's team, he might say something or he might say nothing, leaving you to figure out what you did wrong and for you to correct it. But either way, you'll practice the same scenario twenty times the following day. If you made a mistake on Coach Sal's team, however, he would curse you out in front of everyone. Soon after I joined his team, I made my first error at first base. He pulled me off the field, gave me a very colorfully worded lecture, and someone else sprinted out of the dugout to take my place. There were fourteen very talented players vying for nine spots on the field. My competitive instincts took over, and I made sure to never make the same mistake again.

We were a month out from the Cooperstown tournament and began playing games in Tampa, Florida to prepare. We won every tournament we played. And deservingly so. We had a solid team of very talented, hard-working ball players, several of whom ended up committing to play Division 1 baseball. The problem was, I had only started playing baseball when I was 10 years old, much later than almost everyone else. And although I was a very good pitcher and first baseman, Coach Sal already had his first baseman. If I just pitched, I'd only play once every three or four games, and so Coach Sal also put me in to play shortstop, arguably the hardest position on the field, with the most responsibility.

Even though our team continued to win every tournament, I was not playing too well. I had gotten on base a measly one time, partly because I wasn't getting a lot of playing time, but more importantly because I was off my game. I was 5'11" at the time, taller than everyone else, and when we'd get food as a team or talk to other parents, someone would look at me and ask me how many home runs I've hit, expecting a lofty number I'm sure. And yet every time, my answer was an embarrassing zero. Still, I competed hard at practice and during the games.

Tools Matter

I made it on the team and went to Cooperstown. It's hard to put into words the excitement that surrounds the tournament; the baseball fever, the chatter, the camaraderie, the families, the number of players, the nationalistic identity, the at-capacity hotels – it's an overwhelming experience. It didn't take me long to understand what an incredible opportunity it was to play baseball in the great city of Cooperstown.

Ever since I had started playing, I used a skinny barrel bat. It was the best bat for me, a black and green beauty. Admittedly, I was in a slump, but that was my fault, not my bat's. However, in Cooperstown there are no regulations on what bats you can use, so Coach Sal recommended that I use a big barrel bat instead of my skinny barrel bat. Normally, it'd be the right thing to do. It's a larger bat so I'd have a better chance of hitting the ball. However, I loved my bat. I was comfortable with it. I had hit 7 home runs the spring season before with it. But when you play for Coach Sal, you do what Coach Sal "recommends." The problem, however, was that the big barrel bat was almost dead- yes, that's a real thing. Bats can wane away over time, for example, after hitting a ball 25,000 times, the next 5,000 hits won't be nearly as effective as the first 5,000.

We played a total of nine games, and I ended up getting only 8 at bats. However, I did pitch well. We were a game away from making the Sweet 16 and we were matched against the #1 seed. Like I said, I was almost 6 feet tall at the time, but the monstrous 12-year-olds we played that day had a multitude of players already towering at 6' 4". Remember we were 12 years old! They were hitting 400-feet home runs out of a 200-foot ballpark. Needless to say, we lost that game, which ended our tournament run.

I knew that I wouldn't play with Coach Sal again, so I assumed my Cooperstown experience was a one and done. Out of nowhere, a team from North Carolina got a hold of me. They had seen me pitch and wanted me to play for them. In fact, they had heard about the "Indian kid pitching lights out!" before they had seen me.

I wanted to go back, but I thought it was a long shot. Most teams and players only go once. They experience the city, compete in an electric atmosphere, walk through the historic hall of fame, and make memories that last a lifetime. And then it's over. I was given the unique opportunity in which I could go back with an entirely new team and do it all over again. A few weeks later, and we were back in Cooperstown.

My new Coach was in it for the experience, not to win it. He was a spiritual man who was more of a nice-father than a tough-coach. For example, one of the kids was injured and he still was able to play. Coach Sal would have never let an injured kid step on a field for him. Without the intensity of having to win it all, I got much more playing time and had a greater on-the-field experience.

Unfortunately, our team wasn't very good. The silver lining was that I stood out. I was pitching all the time, and when I didn't pitch, I played shortstop. I hit 3 homeruns and a grand slam in 4 days... with my black and green beauty.

Do it Your Way

People are going to challenge you. No matter what you do there will be others trying to drag you down. With change being an infamously difficult concept to achieve, people don't like watching others accomplish it. Throughout my years of investing, I was told nonstop by both my peers and others who were much older and supposedly wiser that crypto is a joke. They would say, "Save yourself the time and just light your money on fire, you're wasting it away anyway!" But I persisted. As a result, through trials and errors, wins and losses, I slowly began to achieve success.

And this is when, once again, I want to turn your attention to you. Life has not been easy for me. My father walked away from us when I was eight years old; I got ridiculed while playing baseball by coaches, players, and parents; I had enormous losses in crypto. But no one ever said life was supposed to be easy. You can make of life what you desire as long as you are logical, persistent, and patient.

I'd like you to take a moment and answer this question for yourself – after reading this book and understanding the principles that drive investors, having a new understanding of the volatile market that is cryptocurrency, and realizing that research and study will give you a much better advantage than a lucky guess – (and here's the question) – if you put it all together and invested, how do you think your life would look in 12 months?

In chapter 6, I showed you a graph that illustrated how, from July 2020 through July 2021, the S&P 500 went up 42%, which is good. Yet, in that same time frame, Ethereum increased by 1,200%!

Where could you be? What life could you be living? Maybe you've been taking the bus for years... not by choice but by necessity. You'd have enough to buy yourself a nice, dependable car. Maybe you've wanted to diversify in real estate but never had enough for the initial investment. You'd have enough for a sizable down payment. Maybe you're like me and you're interested in getting your pilot's license but then you realized there's a five-figure price tag attached. You'd have more than enough to get up in the air. Maybe you like to travel and take your family on vacations, or maybe you need $25K to buy that new piano that's been on your vision board for years, or maybe you want to taste a bit of luxury and buy that Rolex you've always wanted. It's all right in front of you, you just have to reach out and take it.

In the introduction, I mentioned that the current financial landscape as we know it will be reshaped due to the rapid growth of decentralized finance. If you have children, say a four and two-year-old, and you invest in their names telling them they couldn't touch the money until they're eighteen. You could have enough for their college tuition. All it takes is one strong investment today.

I'll tell you what my mother told me, if you've done the research and you're going to invest, go all in. If the investment turns out to be a winner but it doesn't impact you, you've gone too small. And there's no fun in playing small. You can live the life you design for yourself, but only if you take the initiative.

It's your life. Play your own game. If investing in cryptocurrency feels right to you, take the time to do the research and acquire the skillsets needed to become a prudent and ambitious investor. At the end of the day, if you're like me, you'll be glad to know that no matter what, you followed your own path and you made your own success. Only then will you fully understand the immortal words of the great Frank Sinatra: "I did it my way."

Truthfully, there's no better way to live.

Epilogue

What's Next?

I'd like to thank you for taking your precious time to read my book. It was never my intention to write a book. However, with the convincing of my mother, I took on this amazing endeavor in the hopes that it will positively impact many lives, including yours.

As for me, much has happened between when I started writing and the publication of this book. I'm still putting in three to four hours a day in baseball, playing for the University of Tampa. I'm working towards my ultimate goal of playing at the professional level. Who knows, you may see me walking to the mound in a professional ballpark one day and say, "Hey, isn't That the Crypto Kid?" I don't know whether it'll happen or not, but I'm going for it.

As for the new developments within cryptocurrency since I began this book? It's been absolutely incredible!

I garnered a lot of exposure with my success and have helped many others make money in the industry, some of which you read about, along with many other stories that never made it into this book. I've been featured in the news on TV, in magazines across the country, in newspaper articles, and even radio shows. As a result, many people have wanted me to invest their money for them. That concept is certainly not foreign to me because I grew up watching my mother do it in real estate, and I even dabbled with the exact same business model for quite some time. The good news was that I had access to several million dollars to invest into crypto. The bad news was that I couldn't touch any of it because I didn't have a platform for investing it all.

A conversation between my mother and Preston sparked a brilliant idea - Why not put together a hedge fund? Not just your regular, run-of-the-mill hedge fund, but one that exclusively invests in cryptocurrency.

To lay the proper foundation for context, a hedge fund is a pooled investment fund that trades in relatively liquid assets, and it has the unique ability to make extensive use of complex trading. Through the vehicle of a hedge fund, high net worth individuals and institutional investors can invest in a fund that is specialized toward high-risk, high-reward opportunities. Cryptocurrency is the very definition of high-risk, high reward.

As I started to speak to others about the possibility of me managing a hedge fund that exclusively trades in cryptocurrencies, people bought in. The concept is simple. People would give me substantial amounts of money, and I would choose the crypto investments and manage the fund. I must say, the idea has caught on like wildfire.

To date, my brothers and I have raised more than $10 million in assets under management that will launch the Shembekar Capital hedge fund in 2022. I will soon be the youngest person ever to manage a hedge fund with tens of millions of dollars at only eighteen years old.

I ended this book with the final subheading of the final chapter called Do it Your Way. I didn't write it because I thought it was clever. I wrote it because that's my reality.

There are no guarantees in life, but I know this, you can't hit a pitch if you never step foot in the batter's box.

Now swing away, my friend. Get in there and show the world what you can do!

About The Author

Jackson Royce Shembekar was born on June 5, 2003 to Tushar Shembekar and Anita Jain Shembekar in Tampa, Florida. He is the oldest of three boys, Preston Shembekar and Colin Shembekar. Since the age of 8 years old, he and his brothers were raised by their mother, Dr. Anita Jain Shembekar.

He made his first investment of $20 in cryptocurrency in August, 2017, while a freshman at Jesuit High School, in Tampa. He also played baseball, as a pitcher, and plays the violin, and founded the school's Chess program. By the time he graduated high school, 4 years after his $20 investment, he had grown his portfolio to more than a million dollars.

Jackson is the soon to be portfolio manager of Shembekar Capital, a hedge fund that will trade exclusively with cryptocurrencies. At 18, he will be the youngest person recorded to manage a multi-million dollar fund. His list of clients will include professional athletes, doctors, CEOs, and real estate moguls. The minimum investment will be set at $250,000.

Jackson is also a sought out speaker who specializes in cryptocurrency and real estate investments.

When he's not working out, playing baseball, speaking, or trading, he can be found flying – as he is a certified pilot.

To reach Jackson Shembekar:
Email: jrshembekar@icloud.com
Instagram: @jacksonshembekar
Website: www.thecryptokid.com

NOTES

NOTES

NOTES

NOTES

_____

_____

_____

_____

_____

_____

_____

_____

_____

_____

_____

_____

www.ingramcontent.com/pod-product-compliance
Lightning Source LLC
Chambersburg PA
CBHW032102020426
42335CB00011B/456